*Fenland Winter
and other poems*

ANDREW BRAMWELL

The Choir Press

Copyright © 2025 Andrew Bramwell

All rights reserved. No part of this publication may be reproduced or transmitted in any form or by any means, electronic or mechanical including photocopying, recording or any information storage or retrieval system, without prior permission in writing from the publishers.

The right of Andrew Bramwell to be identified as the author of this work has been asserted by him in accordance with the Copyright, Designs and Patents Act 1988

First published in the United Kingdom in 2025 by
The Choir Press

ISBN 978-1-78963-540-9

Contents

Fenland Winter	2
Here you were made	4
The Face of Joseph	6
Buildwas	9
St. John the Baptist, Cirencester	10
A Personal Geology	12
Awakening	13
Sunrise as Seen from Merton Field	14
What I Am, I Am	15
Ice	16
Journey	17
The Road to the Past	18
When Last I Saw This Land	19
We are all sorry for the spiders death	20
Lupins	21
The Seed	22
Two Leaves	23
New Day	24
Walking through Long Grass	25
Lime Pits	26
Moment	28
Gone	29
Presence	30
Truth is a Hammer	31
The Iron Tree	32
Now Threads the Winter Coverlet	33
Sunrise	34
The Stone	35
An Autumn Stream	36

On Pendle Hill	38
The Uncluttered Room	40
The Orchid Tree	41
Meeting with a Ghost	42
Dover Beach Revisited	45
My Neighbour	46
This is no Africa	47
A Finish War Cemetery – Lappeenranta	48
Saimaa	49
A Moorland Funeral	50
SCHOOL POEMS	53
My spot by the fence	54
School Thoughts	55
School Dinner	56
When Miss Willougby Left	58
Shall we call him John	60
Sharpening a Pencil	62
Our School cat is Percy	64
Dyslexic Tendencies	66
In my box	67
LEAVING KARELIA	69
Leaving Karelia 1940	70

*Fenland Winter
and other poems*

Fenland Winter

The fens are iron slabs,
steeled plates welded to black earth, slammed
down by the press of sky,
rivetted into place by ice nails.

And a north wind shrieks, and
sedged fingers tear breath from brittle
lungs, clasping the throat
in a metallic grip.

Hoar frost cauterizes the eye lid,
lenses burn blurred impressions of
flat fatigue; a merlin
scythes the air like a razor.

Thoughts freeze, solidified
by rime, time passes,
slips or snares, time whispers
 to icicled cheeks, searing red the flesh.

Life unhooks, strips to bone,
like meat dangling from ribs,
carrion.

The fens watch, a mortician's slab,
landscaped alabaster, or marble,
a place of echoes for the dead, dead
flat, uncompromising, deathly quiet,

a half-moon wobble, plasma drips
in the cup of wounds, memories
spark across a corncrake sky, earthly
revolutions too numerous to count elapse.

Snow begins to fall
in holy concealment, smothering lanterns
 in reed beds where the

bittern sleeps. The stone of frosts grip
penetrates, chills, and chides, flakes of onyx pierce
a mind benumbed by cold.

Here you were made

This is where you are made,
a celestial manufacturing plant,
here every nut and bolt,
clamp and lever,
bracket and hinge,
is fixed together.
There is neither concealment
nor deflection,
all out in the open
as it should be.

Here sensation and emotions
are carefully folded,
some replications
from previous generations,
others quite original.
It is a devilishly complex template.
Joy for example is light,
anxiety brittle, perception rare,
courage red, shame … aquamarine.

Now conscience is a tricky one.
Heavy as lead, dense as mercury,
fluid, a rambler.
But on the other hand, contentment
is a mighty gift, a gemstone much pursued …
but rarely captured.
And finally, well love, delicate this.

Love is placed within a pocket
secretly, without a fuss,
you would hardly know it was there.
But it is.
On occasion love is half forgotten,
at other times it slips out of a hole
or hides between a seam.
But if you are really blessed love explodes
SPECTACULARLY.

Now on your way child.

The Face of Joseph

When by chance I turned my head
the face of Joseph held my vision,
an accidental meeting of the eyes,
an acknowledgment of mutual shyness.
He responded with a tender smile, his face
the colour of cedar burned by the sun,
ravaged by a desert wind.

We did not speak at first beyond
polite exchange of greetings; yet
something held him here, a reluctance
to continue with his journey; I
could tell he was unsure,
adjusting his headdress unnecessarily,
twisting the ring upon his finger.

I would have liked to take his arm
in a gentle way; a neighbourly act
of compassion or mutual understanding.
No matter what the thoughts of others
might have been, I saw the patina of grief
enclose this childhood friend of mine,
a truly honest man.

My wife resides still in Jerusalem
he seemed to say, though words did
not express his thoughts, mere sensations
we had shared when boys on Galilean hills,
now as men locked firmly into place.
'Work keeps me here' he said, the subtle
turn of wood, the following of grain.

I almost cried, those depths of feeling ...
sorrow, fear, despair, perplexity, loneliness,
brutally revealed, a carpenter,
a fellow of this dwelled in place,
caught between the cross and nails,
blood and wine, body and bread,
as ... inconsequential as a grain of sand.

Such situations leave me at a loss,
my intentions decent, but clumsy,
anxious not to cause offence; to mask
my foolishness; to snap those
vulnerabilities I try to hide, to erase
misunderstandings. Standing awkwardly
at his side, lost for words.

Then it was in shared bewilderment
I caught the scent of frankincense
carried by the breeze; I saw Joseph
too has picked it up, for his head
stiffened with remembrance, and
for a moment he was lost to me
and all the world.

Flowers with five white petals
floated from the sky, stamens like
a crown of thorns, like a bed of
linen clothed in aromatic oils.
'They say he lives,' he seemed
to say, 'but how can that be?'
Words failed me, as always.

'Sh'lam my friend.'

Buildwas

An arch within an arch,
within an arch, eyebrows
quizzically aligned,
in stone, slabs crafted by
the masons hand, slotted
into place like ribs.
The tower tilts into prayer,
watchful, ruminating, musing,
remembering the brothers,
plainsong, heavenly incense,
steps on chill tiles, chanting,
the wolf howling, a cowl of wind,
rosemary and lemon balm,
cloisters proposing paradise,
lichened walls seared with cold,
with hallucination and mystery,
with the silence of the valley.

St. John the Baptist, Cirencester
(The goblet of Anne Boleyn)

When the first snow fell,
as frost ferned the grass,
and a chill wind stabbed the skin
like axe blades. I saw you shiver
with the cold. Someone just walked
across my grave you said, smiling
wanly.

You passed the silver goblet
into my hands … our fingers touched,
a thrill coursed through my veins,
your humble servant Richard Masters,
as ever in awe, yet touched by a shadow of sadness
and resignation which always followed,
in your steps.

As I recall, a bell rang out, sunlight radiated
beneath a window, crowning your hair,
with white gold.
Then a mirage of your face reflected
in the silver, shimmered as the sea, tearful,
 … with a hint of fear, and our eyes met.

Now Cotswold stone bears witness
to your whispers, haunting, lingering,
strangely linked across the ages.
Incense stokes a reminiscence, carrying
the lips that kissed a king through time.

Yes, we will meet again ...
when the first snow falls.

A Personal Geology

Deep is the time
within the cave that lies
behind your eyes.
A smile, a ripple of electrons
gathered in a thousand-mile whisper.

A pulse – lips quivering in the cold,
breath a cytokine storm pushing …
away the darkness.
Hair swept back by hands
that pushed the button, caressingly.

Time a metered cardiograph
curving distance into …
eternal wakefulness, a millisecond,
an era, a photon swallowed
by the optic nerve, inconsequential
loop of now.

Deep is the time
within the cave that lies
Behind your eyes.

Awakening
(from an illness)

She wakes and notices the window,
a rectangle built into the wall.
Shafts of light penetrate the room

illuminating a tiny yellow flower,
growing in the isolated gloom.
Pollen coats the tips of her fingers.

It seems chains pinning her down
are broken. To a rasp of echoes,
links tumble to the marble floor.

A cloud floats across the sky,
a feather drifts down, a swallow,
or a swift or nightjar.

It drifts like falling snow,
like a fern unfurling,
until she cradles it in her arms.

Sunrise as Viewed from Merton Field

My eye, my eye, is an orange cage, glowing, grated,
    crated into walls gnarled to a blood red core
in thrusts of flayed razor curled edges, serrated,
    like red tipped needles, stapled and
pinned to the inside of the lens, incarcerated,
    my sight spears the photon war, while watching,
it crumples this black earth,
    into blistering birth.

A mess of blood, a flood, a neuron flare
    a sunlit, panoptical revision of Voltaire.
This sunlit massacre of the senses,
    this heart, this core of a sunrise scattered,
this arterial beam, this red light quartered,
    skeletising trees, this dawn, a crimson blade
slaughtering sensations, a detonating fusillade,
    as the atmosphere condenses.

The Cherwell a simmering copper cauldron
    a photonic churn of water, a turn, a hadron
mist hissing silently has spoken.
    Yet still the many layered sky holds sway,
as a summer flight of echoes trails away.
    Like arrows from a candle bird, like the slicing
of amber fruit, the swallow's wing beats splicing,
    a single eyelid open.

What I am, I am

You must take me for what I am
different to you,
Odd possibly ... a matter of opinion!

Caring mostly, certainly unheroic,
often unreasonable
spiteful on occasion ... shamefully.

Cynical regrettably,
Sad at times
in the evening ... sometimes lonely.

Buoyant when the mood takes,
can be excitable
same as everybody else, but different.

Ice

Beneath the ice, a river runs,
slowly or in torrents as may be,
beneath your eyes, a rapid flows,
beguilingly.

Beneath the rime, apparitions glide,
ghosts or spirits twist or flee,
beneath your eyes, a river runs,
alluringly

Journey

It is
a long journey from there to here,
many twists and turns upon the way,
climbs up and down without the benefit
of ropes or ladder, slips, tumbles, an
occasional cartwheel.

It is
a road where hedges burn,
blazing aspirations, smoke smouldering,
eyes smarting, directions choked,
the tunnel of dreams a distant light,
a hand pushing through clouds.

The Road to the Past

The road to the past
is closed, a barricade.
Ivy grows upon the walls,
red bricks fade to brown,
textures are dimmed.

The door to those times
firmly closed, the
key turned, a handle
veneered with rust
and discolouration.

So, the encirclement of time
is complete,
imprisoned if you like,
locked away for our own good,
mostly hidden.

Yet on occasion,
at unexpected times …
a scent, a song, a sense,
a breath of words drifts
daringly across.

Strangely unsettling,
blissful perhaps, unwanted
or sought. The shuttle
runs across the loom,
the thread is made.

When Last I Saw This Land

When last I saw this land
mist curled the slope
in ethereal advance.

Gatherers skimmed heather
gilded by dew, insects crawled
into harebells greedily.

The rams skull sat empty
eyed upon the moor,
long calcified.

Spring rain sparkled,
moisture seeped from
brow to floor.

Silence chimed the breeze
into a melancholy whine,
skin chilled and shivered.

A lone walker on the
skyline, stepped into
the clouds.

We are all sorry for the spider's death

We are all sorry for the spider's death
sorry and sad,
for an eight-legged wonder
… crushed breathless,
by a misplaced boot.
Hardly amusing,
but you have to laugh
don't you?
Such a romantic departure,
like a train pulling from a station.
After all
he had thoughts and dreams too,
responsibility,
up and coming eight legged wonders
crawling, playing in the cabbage,
a web to keep,
uncharted crevices in walls to be explored
… because they are there.
And now
Sir Edmund Hillary Spider
pursues a new career
as a downtrodden blot
on the station platform.

Lupins

The lupins by the fence are
pokers in unfashionable hats,
stiff Victorians with a fondness
for a slightly risqué joke,
or a stand-up comedian
of the lower sort.

The lupins by the fence are
open to all sorts of innuendo,
visually ridiculous in their own way,
the handlebar moustache
of the flowery border,
the red-faced uncle at weddings.

The Seed

In the field of clay
a seed was set
before the war,
when even God was young,
a mere slip of a lad.

A tree grew with a throb and shiver,
a pulse;
breezes licked the branches
in gossamer threads,
singing with the sway of air
like a bow playing a violin.

The trunk became a mast,
spurs the rigging,
leaves green oval sails.
It fancied itself as a clipper on the ocean wide.
But then it knew no better.

Andrew Bramwell: 4 Swan Meadow, Much Wenlock, TF13 6JQ.
bramwellandrew@aol.com

Two Leaves

Two leaves fall
in slow descent,
caressing the air gently,
touching briefly
entwined momentarily,
then separate away.

Both broken by a summer storm
of unusual intensity,
and in the morning calm,
discovered side by side.

A breath of wind
sliced through their bonds,
the merest whisper,
no more than a suggestion.

A nuthatch watched
and turned away.
A spider glanced,
legs trembling.

One accepts
one blindly twists and turns,
earth summons them both.

New Day

A quiet milk-white sky
merges to conifer green,
soft autumn drifts, hay dries
beneath a single Finnish sun.

New salmon clouds rise,
corn lisps, a lake shimmers,
swallows climb in high whispers;
vague hills reverberate to their wings.

From these heights black night retreats,
a liquid melting silently away,
day pours upon the
pastel layered horizon.

Walking Through Long Grass

Walking through long grass,
eyes fixed to the discordant ground,
the swish of green blades; concerto
on a knife edge, sonata
of strings.

At each thundering step
clouds of insects arise
Sir, magisterial projectiles,
the sky a swarm of dots,
flying punctuation marks
wordless and frantic.

When dusk falls, quietly,
a mantle, a shawl, a
gentle quivering; and then
the field is becalmed,
like an empty cradle,
an untenanted cross,
the unset sun.

Lime Pits

A pendulum of footsteps
raise clouds of dust,
the viper curls,
swarms flush,
worlds shrivel and splinter.

Disassembled bones betray
a catch, disarticulated remains.
A woodpecker taps,
oil drops slide upon
the beetles back,
dripping to the floor.

Orchestrations of the dragon fly
unheard by us, our
technologies too crude.
We hear the timpani
but not the harp.

I train myself to listen … to
funnel and filter the colour
of trees, of cochineal,
blistering summer shades,
of life, death, replenishment.

Breath exhales, words
tumble on forest debris
fusing with the sky; green leaves
harness sunlight with the
force of a nuclear explosion.

Blink once and all has gone,
the scene has shifted.
Waters mirror wavering
clouds. Husks and shells discarded,
plaster casts of former life.

Moment

Of this moment
I am only me
and no one else.

One cloud drifting
across the sky,
one blade of grass
swaying in the breeze.

In this moment
the colour of time
is the blue of sky,
a dew drop,
a diamond,
a rainbow,
a spirogyra,
a mirror
and a mask.

Of this moment
I am only me,
and no one else.

Gone

As the front door closes
memories tumble to the floor,
like glass from a frame splintering
a chain of thoughts,
a string of dreams,
filaments
of might have beens.

Beyond the fence
a distant laugh trails
mockingly away.

A magpie croaks,
from tree to tree
claw to claw.

Tears, well tears
cannot be pushed
back into the eye.

 A numbness
crushes; and the walls close,
harsh words bite.
It is all so interminable.

Presence

I have been there,
in that place
where fears dwell.

Under that stone,
or where leaves
fall from tree to floor,
quietly screaming.

But mine was a different stone,
and my forest
was not yours.

So, I know
yet I don't.

Truth is a Hammer

We are all tired, that is the truth,
Gospel.
According to the dictionary truth is a hammer
splintering a door, wood screaming with the blows.
Except that's not true. I made it up.

Truth
is a barbed wave slicing the shore into granular smiles,
like grit in the iris, an uncomfortable, irreversible experience,
a kind of swelling. The truth is you cannot push tears back
    into the eyes.
That may be true or just a dream I had one unsettled night,
when my weariness was real or not. A grey area.

Truth
Rips ... and yet sooths like those shadow spilling silences
    you hear about, or not.
Moments of consummation and dreamy awareness, as if
    some interloper has
entered your head and stirred with a spoon.

Truth
Tilts the edges of the windowpane so sunlight streams into
    every corner of the room.
It eludes your grasp but leaves residual warmth, like a
    long-hidden fossil,
except a fossil is a million, million times cold.
Truth is atonement they say.

The Iron Tree

The gnarled tree
  contorted,
    twisted in grimace,
      distorted by wind and rain,
        planed by ice, sliced, enlaced
          as vicissitudes of climate
            scooped and hollowed and rimed,
              an aged face stooped; beyond
                a century or more of grind.

                Misshapen; persecuted even,
            embellished features
           tortured into resonances
          relished by skeletons.
        Enamelled, frosted into elegance
        but still, still, still here, still
        hanging on, an earthly Orion
      unbreakable, steeled, riveted,
    A grip of iron.

Now Threads the Winter Coverlet

Now threads the winter coverlet
over rock pools icing the moon's glow,
in skies where planets are scarce
and thoughts rarer still.
In heavens where clouds
bob sail boats.

Now too threads the cloth of winter
where bay winds tip and fold,
and waves list gently, rolling
in the equinox that breezes
carry still as songs
in sixpences.

Now weaves the thread of winter,
through windows of summer cottages
low nailed, salted
by the ripples of shores long
looped in sprays
of sea holly.

Now finally threads the winter coverlet,
spidering channels scooped only
in ribbon, wracked
only by lanyards of wars
lost loves
in days stolen.

Sunrise

Orange glowed to a volcanic core,
razor curled edges, ripped red,
red tipped, blasting a black earth,
flaming breath, an enraged insurrection.

Flares scorch skeletal willow,
branches splinter, leaves shred,
the fruit of morning falls, a
summer flight of wings departs.

Skyways flow lava streams,
magna explodes, the world tingles,
horizons whisper and yawn,
the sun resurrects, eyes open.

The Stone

This stone I found beside the road,
an ordinary road, out of town.
a marlstone rounded by the wind,
gnarled by sun and frost,
carried here by persons unknown.

A crust of clay or silt
bedevils the surface, clumps
break away, grains combine
and split, shatter, slither
to the ground.

But the precious core is shielded,
packed with jewels of
every kind and shade. Some
transparent, more opaque, most blind,
both priceless and without worth.

Here dwells fear and love,
regrets, mistakes, triumphs, desire,
memories both lost and stolen,
all entwined … trapped. I scoop
it in my arms and carry it away.

Autumn Stream

Light departs now,
twilight beckons; an early star
stirs the amber laden steam
to a broth of distortion.
Two worlds are polarised,
below, burst suns
flatten and yellowise.

above,
insects struggle on the surface,
wings entrapped, compound eyes
scanning desperately.
This river is an old net,
ancient as a druid.

The soft ripple of chalk water
hums her tail; soothes, reminds,
recalls instinct and memory.
The riverbed sparkles
iridescent with horizontal sunlight.
Tiny pebbles clink together
kissing gently.

Gravel moans across the floor,
tilting this way and that
with the flow.
From a recess a shivering
of water cress, a hair of
mid channel crowfoot,
caresses her scales.

The scampering white clawed cray fish,
lamprey, a caddis fly nymph
all visible within her field of vision.

Soft water calls,
alder leaves glide across the surface.
Moonlight begins to stretch
in icy fingers across her body.
There is a gentle settling of another
day, a yawn, a fin shiver.

On Pendle Hill

How the snow glistened,
how stars fell like pearls
from a sky rich in blue,
and crows flew across the face
of the moon in quiet formations.

A wingless flurry of air
caressed my skin,
eyes glowed in lenses misty.

How horizons sucked land
to sky; melting one into the other,
elevating my body, arms like cherry rods.
A slow advance of light calibrated
in metronomic fingers,
pointing.

Then whispers …
'I have heard your voice so many times
in the stillness; in the splash of water
when the oars are working,
in dim passages of days,
in water falling from the swallows
wing; in boughs
of an apple tree shading Adam
from the sun.

I will follow you
beyond the lairs of demons,
through forests rich in pine and fir
and silver birch.

I will follow when the magpies chattering
fades from gold.
to topaz.

When the salmons leap
gilds frost to stone,
I will be your guide.'

The Uncluttered Room

The room bears no hint of shade,
no shadow or silhouettes,
just square white walls
and bare windows peeling light,
from the desert outside.

A space illuminated by fierce suns
spinning photons, driving sand
onto the ledges like malignant leprosy.
A shivering haze licks the horizon outside,
arid, empty, nothingness.

Bare ceilings and naked boards
conjure images I know, are not there,
a kind of blindness through which light
pours unseen, an invisible Satre
reading spirit, unclothed.

The Orchid Tree

There is no such thing as an orchid tree,
but if there was, it would be,
a sparkling chandelier on the banks
of a river looped down vales,
an aqueous bracelet with a mind,
of its own.

There is no such thing as an orchid tree,
but if there was, it would be,
an elongated vein cusping hearts
and pinecones, acorns, and sycamore
helicopters, jewelled leaves, the
pulse of earth.

There is no such thing as an orchid tree,
but if there was, it would be,
the haunt of silver ghosts rustling
in the breeze, a stand of lanterns
smiling away darkness, a
hope beacon.

Meeting with a ghost

A chance encounter brought me here,
some kind of dream meeting laced with vertigo,
consummated with no words.
A dark coat collar, gloved hand occasion …
yet more dead of night, glare of the moon
in lunar light, a silvered finger
seeming to point me out.

A car glides past,
an echo of sounds tumbles to the floor,
reverberations and tremors; I fold my arms
across my chest like wings.
Cold air lances my forehead.

Hush these windows, harbour eyes
Irised with malignancy
Luminous with venom,
They are watching you,
Time is nothing.

Old Victorian alleys, black as caves
hide beckoning fingers,
foreshadowing temptation.

And where once bombs fell
paper drifts across a corncrake cloud.
Streetlights flicker to
the burnished wings of moths,
a world in monochrome.

I stand solitary and exposed.
Narrow streets throttle my thoughts
like a kraken.

A pigeon flaps, rats scurry,
a muted violin plays some ghostly tune
and fades away, away, away.

I twitch with fear and think to turn
and walk away before these city stones
may rivet my feet.

But then she comes, footsteps soft,
shoelaces flapping on the cobbles,
an ominous arrival.

'You are here''
'I am'.
She nods.

A dog howls. I shiver.

'This is the furnace of hell.
The clanging, clamouring, cauldron,
the meat grinder,
the besmircher,
the incinerator.'

I could not speak.
A chill ran down my spine' some
primeval terror awakened.

She laughed quietly, touching my hand.
'When last we met, your last breath,
elapsed with pale gasps
and led you here.'

These walls, these streets, these chimneys,
the sulphurous air, the iron and steel,
the brass and zinc and copper,
the acid, these I leave to you.
They are your birth right. A solemn bequest.
Here your forbears laboured and succumbed,
the bricks claw you for their own.
You are theirs. It is so.
You are the ghost, not I.'

Dover Beach Revisited

The sun is calm tonight, she fades
like the final glimmers of a candle bird,
like silver glass splintering from a frame,
fresh shards scattered in sharp alignments.

Paper tumbleweeds across the shingle shore,
pebbles kiss and part with the falling tide,
one cheek naturally, not the continental two.
A ferry sinks into the horizon,

sea green as cellulose, sky a shepherd of clouds.
It seems as if...
I stand on tip toe, peering through a wall invisible
towards a Doggerland scattered with flint,

antler horn, amber beads, Mesolithic keepsakes.
such is the power of remembering. This tingle
of waves was once, was once my favourite song,
was once nebulously twisted into memories, once.

My Neighbour

You are my neighbour, but I do not know you.
You are a shadow slipping away, a sleight of hand
as the door closes; your footsteps padding
upon the concrete path. I notice you wear sandals
even on the coldest, darkest, winter days.

I must admit to some gentle curiosity
as to your origins; the long, long road
which carried your African soul beyond my window.
I wonder why you would exchange the burning sun
for this dismal monochrome.

Sometimes I hear the muffled ocean
of your language trickle through my walls,
or like raindrops, exploding with the intensity
of a tropical monsoon. Sometimes,
yes, sometimes I would like to speak with you.

I imagine your heart beats to the rhythm
of the tambele and bala, and mentally at least,
your nights are still tormented by the drone
of mosquito's, not the lumpen blue bottles
that litter our soggy windowsills.

I wonder if you share your thoughts
beneath the dreamy stars like me,
not in a prayer exactly, but as a form
of timid hopefulness. If only, if only
we could understand each other.

This is no Africa

It is not like the rain of home
bulleting on tin roofs with volcanic intensity,
maker of red mud.
This relentless drizzle
 is a worm slithering down the wall,
gorged on fat.

And as I close the door, dust settles.
A spider crawls across the carpet,
on legs like an apostrophe overdosed on ink
punctuating the floor,
incorrectly.

Even trains squelch boringly in this place,
unlike the dragon breath of old steam
lovingly bequeathed
by our colonial masters.

Outside a black bird stands dripping on the fence,
contemplating pneumonia.
There are no honey buzzards here
soaring to a blistering sun,
this is no Africa.

A Finnish War Cemetery – Lappeenranta

Here we lie
the dead who will not awake
when earths quaking ceases,
and the final homeward waves have rolled
ashore in fits and peaces.
We are the corpse brother, the stench you covered
with soil, the eyes you closed,
the lips you kissed, the body you buried.

We rest,
the dead who did not learn
to turn and walk away,
when the spade had ceased its swallowing
our lips in clay.
We are the sacks, the meat you carried
away on a cart, the skull you shovelled
the hair you combed, the village boys.

Saimaa

Rowing Saimaa …
songbirds hidden in reeds,
eyes in bulrushes,
shadow watching,
glimmer catching,
alert.

Arms exercised
like water boatmen,
vision hunting,
sparkle chasing,
excited.

Cold hands
ripple enveloped,
mist roped,
cloaked furtively.

Thoughts rising
sounds fading, notes
sinking. A gentle splash,
eternity.

A Moorland Funeral

Footsteps sink a thousand tombs.
Our crashing through mauve heather rips the wind
in wondrous thunder.
Boots more accustomed to ploughing fields
than uncomfortable ritual
trample and bruise the earth.

The graveside yawns, a mouth opens
ready to receive.
Soil covers the old man's cells.
He succumbs piecemeal, a sad rose,
and the ice in fern folds bends, hovering
over the hole in limp blades; white
feather frost lingers, the air brittle
and scentless. Our breath a ghostly miasma.

Aye
it is he.
He who once walked yonder hills
and dwelt among the longhouses,
a pale bud of a man.
His cottage sucked the slope like a limpet,
wind screamed through the rafters,
firelight tigered his walls … smoke drifted
from the chimney, from then to now.

So
all this we remember.
We mourners grinding snow grasses
underfoot,
eyes descending; and on yonder hills
which once he walked
crisp, clear clouds like an orange bay
caught my eye, while soil sank blind
his cancerous body.

School Poems

My spot by the fence

This is my spot by the fence,
just left of the drain,
facing the boiler house door,
where the wind screams
round the corner.
An oasis of calm in the yard
I don't think!
Not much of a view, grey mostly,
a puddle here and there
half a worm.
That's why I'm here
by the fence, again.

Barry said I'd eaten the other half,
RIDICULOUS!
I don't deal in fractions.
So, this is my play time
punishment … standing.
I'm allowed to scratch discretely,
but that's about it.
Long arm of the lunch time supervisor
pointed me here,
no playing or talking,
no roistering,
just loitering without intent.
'Best of it is,' she said
'You didn't eat your dinner!'

School Thoughts

School makes you brainy as a fish finger.

Reading is a mysterious conjuring trick.

Assemblies are like giant sleep overs in a big room.

A tyrannosaurus rex reminds me of a certain dinner lady.

Learning times tables is like walking on skulls.

When the work is difficult it is a tunnel of cobwebs.

Playing with a skipping rope opens a world of possibilities.

When the playground grass is mown let there be heavenly battles.

School Dinner

The potato on my plate has a face,
not necessarily beautiful or handsome,
but a face all the same.
Soft caramel skin marked here and there
with attractive pimples,
an unfunny lopsided grin,
two sad eyes.

'Don't eat me' it said.
I was taken aback and
scanned the dining hall carefully,
to see if anyone else had heard.
'Please don't eat me', it pleaded.
There was the slightest shudder
of fear; unusual for a vegetable.

What was I supposed to do?
Potatoes were being devoured
left, right and centre on every table.
'Escape quickly,' I whispered,
hoping my voice had not carried above
the background hum.

'I am not a boy,' it said.
'I cannot run like the wind or jump and
spring.
I am all body and carbohydrate.'
'And a few lumps,' I added unhelpfully.
There was a sigh.
'Please.'

Some children were mashing
them up with forks.
Then Big Joe looked across.
He was big for a reason.
'I'll have that if you don't want it.'
He speared the potato with a fork,
swallowed whole, in one,
just like that.
'Well,' I thought 'Well.'

When Miss Willougby Left

When Miss Willougby left, it felt as if the trees had lost their leaves.
We had expected her to be an ever present,
after all she had been here since the war, which war it was I can't recall.
She seemed to be our very own Victorian, an embodiment of that era,
though of course she couldn't have been.

This had been her classroom, 'Acme Thunderer' on the desk,
box of chalks at the ready, none of these new-fangled whiteboards.
Always a vase of flowers, daffodils in Spring, a tulip or two,
and a nature table following the seasons year by year, generation by generation.

Christmas dinner in school she said, was the highlight of her year.
Even the handle of the playground bell moulded to the shape of her hand.
I always looked for the lime green cardigan, bobbing with that bird like gait
down the polished corridor floor, hoping she wouldn't slip,
but she never did. In her younger days she must have been a skater.

Miss Willougby was a kind of midwife, bringing us into the world,
the pristine and the grubby, the clever and the not so ...
I half expected to hear her tinkling on the piano,
 'All things bright and beautiful
 All creatures great and small,'
or the classroom prayer at the end of the day.

Now she has disappeared into solitary retirement.
We gave her a card and a painting
of a budgerigar, like her Wilmot.
She said she would miss us
and I knew she was telling the truth.
It was not just the usual words.
She was at retirement age she said. Well past it actually.
The powers that be claimed she had fulfilled her duty
for half a century. She deserved a rest.

I saw her close the door, carrying an umbrella and a carrier of gifts.
When she waited at the bus stop, I saw her glance towards the playground railings,
the call of children must have carried from the past.
I wondered how she felt, after all those years.
At that moment in time the meaning of sadness ...
was brought home to me.
The bus trundled down the lane
I waved, she smiled distantly,
I hoped she would make it.

Shall we call him John

Shall we call him John,
for I forget his name,
age about eight,
short of stature,
short blonde hair,
wouldn't say boo
to a goose.

Rarely said boo
to anything,
it was a school rule
you see,
Head didn't like it.
Boo was a no no..
definitely.

Then one day
in literacy,
subordinate clauses
or something
rather interesting,
he reacted to it
individually.

There he stood
by the sticker chart,
behind the smiley faces,
all grinning fixedly,
except him; he
did not move,
not a muscle.

Stood stock still,
feet together,
arms to the side,
smartly to attention,
like a miniature
Foggy Dewhurst,
strange.

No manner of threat
no coaxing,
no ridicule or bribe
would shift him,
for hours on end,
a tower of boyhood,
Rigid!

John you've missed
your playtime,
silly boy, and now
the gravy has solidified
on your plate, the custard
dried to a scab,
Yuck.

Reason could not move,
nor friendly appeals,
the pencil Robert
shoved surreptitiously,
up his nose, merely
gave him an unusual
profile.

What a puzzle,
it was no condition,
no mysterious syndrome,
as far as the psychologist
could tell. No sign of
nits said the nurse,
scratching.

John's parents came,
nice couple, very normal,
he owned a garage,
she permed her hair
and cried into a handkerchief.
Whatever will become
of our John?

He will have to go,
our Feng Shui is
seriously disturbed.
The Head said this
very, very seriously.
So, he was carried to the car,
underarm, like a plank.

Sharpening a Pencil

If I had to name my favourite thing at school,
it would not be geometry, or poetry or the history
of dead people, or the hell of play time.
Not standing in a smart straight line
in the freezing cold until everybody is ready,
except Sam, for whom an exception is made.

Certainly not the 'be good' assembly,
bad is better, nor fire drills,
nor the miserable school photographer
who hates children.
It would be sharpening a pencil because …

Sharpening a pencil is like infinity and beyond,
  A thing of beauty, a joy for ever,
    A labour of love,
  Ask not what your pencil can do for you
But what you can do for your pencil.

Our School Cat is Percy

Our school cat is Percy,
he is always
slipping through the fence at play time,
soliciting the occasional pat,
nibbling a crisp here or there,
chicken flavour preferably,
or at a pinch smoky bacon.

Percy our school cat
holds one end of a skipping rope,
smiling widely, a self- satisfied grin
on his rugged face,
knowing himself to be
ABSOLUTELY INDESPENSIBLE!
Everyone says so.

Percy our school cat
is the janitor's special friend,
keeps a furtive look out
when a cigarette is needed
behind the coal bunker … boys toilets again
WHAT DO THEY DO IN THERE?

Percy our school cat
can keep the rodent population down
if required, if you ask nicely,
and can spare some toast, nicely buttered.
He can even catch the livelier year ones,
and drop them at Miss Roberts feet
like a mouse. Doesn't feature
in our behaviour policy,
but effective.

So, when the home time bell
rings merrily away,
Percy our school cat does
a little skip, peace at last,
winks suggestively, slyly even,
licks his paws, curls into a ball
and sleeps all night in his own
personal, not to be disturbed
lost property basket.

Dyslexic Tendencies

'So, he has dyslexia.'
'Dyslexic tendencies actually.'
'Will he live?'
Will it shorten his life?
Will he still be able to have children?

We had such high hopes,
now he'll end up being a teacher
or something; maybe a social worker
and we so wanted him to be on X Factor.

Never mind dear heart
I'm sure there are tablets we can
purchase from the internet; or
a clinic in America which can facilitate
a cure; Lets go home now and tell Auntie Vi.'

In my box

In my box I will place,
tiny feet,
dancing jellybeans,
blue leaves,
a flying eagle
a breath of wind,
tornados,
Space (all of it),
the last bounce,
the gentle push of a tricycle,
a hamster with muscles,
a few electrons,
nits (obviously my own).

Leaving Karelia

Leaving Karelia 1940

Walking on ice, the ice of the night
is akin to walking on razor blades.
Ruts and channels slice through leather, and
contort the feet no matter how well protected.
It is a slow, painful process,
the earth is a ghost of polarised light.

There is no colour, black and white and grey
and silver from the moon, that is all.
Sound is amplified.
The sickening shell and skull crushing crackle
as boots fall and wheels turn
arouse satanic shivers.

All frequencies and wavelengths combine,
assault the ear drums with the pattering's of spite.
Soon cold numbs all feeling. A journey of minutes
in this deep world, is spun into agonising hours.
Then truth strikes like a hammer on an anvil,
ripping the body apart and exposing all flesh.

It is as if some unjust punishment descends,
vandalising all that was once familiar.
In that quiet dark time sins splatter the soul,
real and imagined, all regrets and sorrows,
all apologies and atonements, words and consummations
gush into the hollows bored by anxiety.

This slows you. This causes the brain to solidify,
and muscle to curl. All you can do is keep moving,
there is no choice, no backward glances, no wondering
at divine punishment. Eyes on the road, concentration,
no falls, or slips, this is neither the time nor place
for broken bones.

The station wears a muffled light, wary of raids,
for the sky is a rich sapphire blue, the cold bitter,
stars shine and planets complete their orbits.
Everyone is here, all hearth neighbours,
all farmstead dwellers, unloading from cart and mind.
Humanity in knots ...

Tuija rolls the barrow to the platform, she sighs.
Little Merja rests on piles of luggage, watches all,
misses nothing, who knows what she makes of the scene,
weariness etched into her features, carved with a knife.
Awaiting orders, wait, wait with fearful patience,
the dictatorship of thoughts, wordless.

All massed in that place wonder, what if,
what if the train does not arrive, wonder at their destination,
wonder at the spatter of small arms fire spitting
from the east, the land of devils. So, farmer, woodsman,
grave digger wait, nerves shredded, hearts seeping
onto the platform. What if?

This is one of many temporary displacements.
There is a determination to be stoical. Yet what if?
What if the train does not arrive? Is this waiting wise?
Mrs. Juutilainen could not rest. Leaving Merja, Tuija,
she leaves the platform overflowing, laced with ice,
into the goods yard grown beside the tracks.

Coal lies heaped, timber, drums of oil,
a coverlet of snow buries them ... how ordinary.
How the warehouse door screams and protests, yet,
yet almost empty. In the pale moons glow, secrets,
silver light bounces across the floor, chill reflections
directing the eye towards the window.

She sees a line of four pine coffins, catches her breath.
Names scrawled hurriedly in pencil on the lids,
Private ... Corporal ... Rifleman ...
'You shouldn't be in here Mistress.' The station masters voice
echoes and reverberates in that holy place.
Their glazed eyes meet in dull bewilderment.

'This is no place for a woman,' he whispers softly.
'Who are they?'
'Lads from the front. Came in from Viipuri this morning.
All day I have been here, when duties allowed,
what a day it has been too.'
Words float upon the air, breath condenses.

'Where are they going?'
'Onwards'.
Documentation is missing, too many coffins,
the front too close for formalities,
disorder and the devil rule now, there
is no escaping a miserable tide.

'When first they came, I thought,
my lad might be amongst them,
lost him yesterday you know.'
'I'm sorry to hear that sir.'
'When his mother knows it will shatter
her to pieces, into a million shards.

Demons danced around him, mocking,
taunting, hissing, pulling at his fob,
tilting the peak of his railway cap,
shrieking were they, revelling, rejoicing
in his pain, contorting their faces into
comedic masks, exhaling foul breath.

To all he was oblivious, he noticed no barbs
of spite. But the mother did, she observed with rage
red devils with claws like pincers, voices rasping
with malevolence. She called upon the angels, summoned
down prayers, and incantations ... and the demons
sank screaming and jabbering into the floor.

'She has a right to know.'
'Yes, so she has … but not yet.
I have not the courage.' And his eyes scan
the warehouse walls, and his breath a haze
of vapour pours out his soul. Her tears
are unrestrained and flow in rivers.

'Such a waste mistress, such shocking waste.
How we sow our seeds and the Lord in his mercy
harvests the fruit. Such a good lad, our only child,
and his mother dreaming of grandchildren as women do.
It will break her heart.' Then the wind blows,
a door bangs, and they shudder.

'I can stay for a while says she.'
'No Mistress the train will soon arrive,
as far as I know it is on time. When it pulls into
the platform, walk to the rear carriage,
stay by the door, it is an easier escape if
needs must. His eyes see through her presence.

Chances are planes will attack at some point …
if they do, wait for the train
to stop, don't try to jump while it moves.
Then rush for the trees, you will be quite safe there.
What is this madness thinks she,
Where has it come from?

Keep your eyes open, try to be ready.'
'I will, thank you.' How did it come to this?
How did it come to this?
How did it come to this?
She turns for the exit, touching the coffins
with her fingers, whispering a goodbye prayer.

'I hope you find your boy.'
'So, do I Mistress.'
'God Bless.'

She walks back to the platform.
Steam rises from an engine, a dragon, a serpent,
humming moodily, impatient to escape.
The crowd shuffles forward, anxiety etched,
no carved, no bayonetted on their faces
in frantic inertia, prayers fly like projectiles.

Clutching Merja tight in one hand and a suitcase
in the other, she forces open the carriage door.
Tuija follows, stows the remaining baggage,
onto racks, it is a tight fit, boxes and bundles
stacked in mocking heaps, someone quietly cries,
women and children and old men brace their thoughts.

From the window Russian prisoners under guard,
shuffle miserable away like parcels unravelling.
She captures every second, tries to place this moment
in a pocket, but it seeps away as the blank eyed
station master waves his flag and blows his whistle.
The train strains, tears flow, thoughts capsize.

The winter solstice stretches fingers forward,
Silence descends. What is there to say?
'Where we are going, do you know?' Tuija asks.
'Away, away, away, away, away.'
'She tucks Merja's hair beneath her woollen hat,'
it is always fleeing; such is the way of things.

'Don't take off your boots, either of you,
make sure you are not entangled,
I have the handle of the door. If we need to,
we can escape in seconds. If we need to, wait for the train
to stop and run for the trees. Don't look back. Throw
yourself down'.
Westwards ran the train, carriage lights were dimmed.

www.ingramcontent.com/pod-product-compliance
Lightning Source LLC
LaVergne TN
LVHW041308080426
835510LV00009B/906